CONTENTS

INSTITUTE OF EDUCATION
UNIVERSITY OF LONDON

Published by

the Tufnell Press

THE LONDON FILE - PAPERS FROM THE INSTITUTE OF EDUCATION

PUBLISHED

by

the Tufnell Press

47, Dalmeny Road, London, N7 0DY

First published 1992

BRITISH LIBRARY CATALOGUING-IN-PUBLICATION DATA

A catalogue record for this book is available from the British Library

ISBN 1 872767 11 7

Book design by Fiona Barlow, Carter Wong, London

Printed in Great Britain by Da Costa Print, London

MUSIC EDUCATION AND THE NATIONAL CURRICULUM

THE LONDON FILE - PAPERS FROM THE INSTITUTE OF EDUCATION

Titles in the series include:

WHAT WE KNOW ABOUT EFFECTIVE PRIMARY TEACHING	Caroline Gipps
MORE HAS MEANT WOMEN: The feminisation of schooling	Jane Miller
THE ARTS 5-16: Changing the agenda	John White
THE RIGHTS OF THE CHILD: Educational implications of the United Nations Convention	Susan Wolfson
CHARTERS, CHOICES AND EDUCATIONAL RESPONSIBILITIES	Anthony Green
NATIONAL CURRICULUM SCIENCE: So near and yet so far	Arthur Jennings
THE PROMISE AND PERILS OF EDUCATIONAL COMPARISON	Martin McLean
THE AIMS OF SCHOOL HISTORY TEACHING: Has the National Curriculum got it right?	Peter Lee, John Slater, Paddy Walsh and John White
TENSIONS IN TEACHER TRAINING	Clare Hake
EDUCATION AND EMPLOYMENT	Michael Young

Music education before the National Curriculum

In this paper I want to explore the general curriculum setting, the evolution of music as part of the National Curriculum and the status of music as a school subject, before analyzing the major theoretical assumptions that frame these perspectives. My intention is to clarify the current position and indicate where future developments may lie.

There are several existing characteristics of British music education which make up the context of music in the National Curriculum. Until fairly recently, music educators had a tendency to be professionally inarticulate; preferring a non-explicit attitude to a declared curriculum statement, getting on with organising and teaching and leaving school, local education authority and national policy formulation to others. Encouraged by the soft-edged attitudes of the 1960s we have tended to favour what is sometimes called the 'process' model, rather than the sharp definition of instructional objectives. However vague this might appear, there is a profound truth here, beautifully and simply expressed by Polanyi in his famous phrase, 'we can know more than we can tell'.[1] Much knowledge may indeed be *tacit*: we do know more than we can tell, or indeed want to be bothered to tell. This luxury of the undeclared; the hidden curriculum, the 'secret garden', is now being invaded by educational accountants who want to know what it is we actually buy and sell and at what price. Music educators are now more articulate, although this burgeoning eloquence is unlikely totally to displace the intuitive sense that characterises the musician's view of musical encounters. Teachers of music are particular committed to their 'subject' as an intrinsically rewarding activity. While they may worry about the plodding predictability of a linear curriculum with check-lists of chained, sequential competencies, it is only fair that *all* children in school have the chance to be initiated into musical procedures, the realm of musical discourse, in a manner less haphazard than reliance on the idiosyncrasies of individual teachers. This, presumably, is one major purpose behind the National Curriculum.

In many ways music education in Britain compares well with other countries, even though it is somewhat erratic. Seen from a comparative perspective attitudes seem generally well-principled, though it is uneven in practice. It is in the schools that this is strikingly apparent. Music in higher education, particularly in universities and music schools, has models and replicas in other parts of the globe; though even at this level, the growth of courses in polytechnics and colleges of higher education has generated new course structures and helped to loosen up the processes of music education for adults. But it is mostly in the schools that pioneering developmental work has taken place. Unfortunately the effects are distributed somewhat unevenly.

The profession has absorbed the effects of the theory and practice of various curriculum initiatives, especially the Schools Council project, *Music in the Secondary School Curriculum*, which began to be influential two decades ago.[2] There was an early advocacy of a serious regard for Afro-American musics, especially jazz and pop music.[3] Many of us have been at work trying to establish a credible and serviceable philosophy of music education and have laboured to tease out the psychological and sociological characteristics of musical experience in order to evolve sound working principles for the classroom and the studio.[4] Eventually it was the GCSE national criteria and the detailed format of GCSE examinations that signalled official acceptance of much that had been pioneered before. Throughout this process Her Majesty's Inspectorate followed along behind, mopping up the ideas and commending 'good practice'.

Consider the range of activities already to be found in school music classrooms. Between 1985 and 1987, the Music Department of the Institute of Education conducted an enquiry into music in schools. Supported by the Gulbenkian Foundation, the aim of this research was to map out the context and practice of music teaching in a wide range of school classrooms and examine the role of music within the wider school community. The research method was by survey and case study. This study gives a picture of attitudes to music in schools and the reality of classroom transactions. It serves as a marker by which to assess the likely impact of proposed change under the novelty of the National Curriculum.[5]

The findings from this investigation suggest that the situation was not then so very different from what is now being proposed. The main divergence lies in the 'national' formulation of curriculum content, rather than leaving all decisions to individual schools and teachers. The actual structure and status of the music curriculum before legislation is not markedly dissimilar from what is now being proposed.

Music was part of the curriculum in every school we investigated, at least until the age of fourteen, with a usual allocation of one period a week which could vary between 20 and 80 minutes. Generally speaking, the younger the pupils the shorter the available time. Amongst the staff of school communities, music was perceived as being quite highly valued; certainly by heads and other teachers, caretakers, secretaries, librarians and other ancillary staff. Many music teachers also thought that their professional contribution to the general life of the school was significant and were aware of the importance of music in helping to project a positive institutional image. In spite of this recognised and much appreciated 'window dressing', music teachers seemed uncertain, even defensive, about their own standing within the timetabled curriculum. They identified a professional requirement to justify their subject and felt classroom work in music was not properly understood by many colleagues. Music as a 'subject' seemed to languish in status by being perceived as 'unacademic', pleasurable rather than educational. A growing vocational emphasis also appeared to exert a strong pull against arts subjects and this affected the major resources of time, space, equipment and staffing. Two-thirds of the 60 teachers involved in this study thought they were more or less inadequately resourced.

When we looked carefully into the classrooms we found a recurring picture. In the primary schools there was an emphasis on aural and performance skills: imitating rhythms; learning patterns on percussion accompaniments by rote; listening games; identifying metre or the number of notes in a chord; responding to changes in levels of loudness and learning new songs. This kind of activity accounted for nearly 51 per cent of the total teaching time observed in primary schools. Nine per cent of the overall time was spent in discussion and classroom organisation and 18 per cent in other ways, including 14 per cent lost in moving children around the school. No significant amount of time was recorded spent on imparting information about music, giving historical, social context or technical facts.

This last trait was also evident in secondary schools, where only 2.5 per cent of the time was taken up by teachers in transmitting information. Nearly 18 per cent of the duration of music sessions was employed in individual, pair, group or whole class composing, half of this 'by ear' (that is to say, without using any form of written notation). About 9.5 per cent of available time was given over to music audience-listening and 22 per cent to rehearsing skills, while 6.7 per cent was taken up in musical performance.[6]

Half of the 7.8 per cent performance time in primary schools saw the children engaged in singing. In the secondary schools the emphasis was much more on instrumental work. A major difference in emphasis became evident across primary and secondary schools, the former making much more of sequential skill teaching and singing in whole classes while the latter engaged more in instrumental performance and composing in small groups.

The belief that music should be a practical subject is, then, already generally accepted by teachers and the desirability of this is stressed in the National Curriculum Music Working Group Report.[7] In answers to our initial questionnaire, teachers from 48 of the 60 schools in the survey reported spending half or more of their time organising practical activities. Subsequent detailed observation in classrooms suggested that this may well be an underestimation. One thing became clear; relaying factual information *about* music was an insignificant feature in all 32 schools that we followed up by systematic observation and interviews. In comparison with other subjects, pupils too had noticed that in music there were 'no paper and pencils', and 'more movement than writing'.

The Working Group strongly advocated singing as an essential part of music education and lists it repeatedly as an activity throughout the Key Stage statements. On the surface this already seems part of practice. More than two-thirds of our respondents claimed that singing was the most frequent classroom activity and 13 that it occurred fairly often. It was indicated that in no school was singing ignored, though two of the teachers involved specified that singing took place only rarely. Even sight-singing appears to flourish. In only 15 instances were there teachers who said they never asked pupils to sing at sight from notation, while 17 teachers said that this took place fairly often. Subsequent observations of 163 lessons in 32 of these schools painted a somewhat different picture. Ninety one of these lessons involved no singing at all. Nor was any sight-singing observed. This is probably a good example of aspirations outstripping actuality. On singing there is a clear difference between the newly proposed and existing curriculum practice. In reality vocal activities have a low position as a classroom activity and the music Working Group was aware of this.

The Group was anxious not to confine musical experience in schools to the western classical tradition. Indeed, in their Interim Report they appeared to get their examples of various musical styles slightly out of balance and a small but vociferous group of academics critical of current developments in music education were quick to respond in the press. This balance appears to have been restored in the final version, but there is no sense in which western classical music is to be an exclusive cultural locus. As far as existing practice goes, we found mainly European idioms, along with less easily classified songs and carols, most frequently cited by teachers. However, there was considerable variation between individuals, some never presenting classical music, others never using jazz, rock and pop, or 'ethnic' music, although most people operated a broad curriculum.[8] The use of available published materials was equally diverse, over 130 different titles were mentioned. Nearly everyone devised their own material. No one appeared to follow a published 'method'. Until now the music curriculum has definitely been homespun.

There is a further practical dimension to be considered. In Britain we inherit two traditions of music education, especially in secondary schools. The first of these derives from the private school system and essentially sees the music educator as the 'director of music' who runs the band, choir and orchestra, who manages the chapel choir and organises individual instrumental teaching. The second tradition stems from the framework of the class lesson where music is treated like any other 'subject' with allocated slots of time for general music education. In most schools the two systems run side by side, with instrumental teaching engaged on a rota basis, withdrawing students from other classes to work with visiting specialist teachers. The regular music teacher wears both hats, that of musical director and class teacher, coping with classes all day and rehearsals, performances and instrumental administration in spare moments and after school. The strain is enormous but difficult to avoid. Teachers feel that the classes are the real reason for their employment and yet the choirs, bands and orchestras are necessary, not only to put the music department on the map of the school in the eyes of staff and parents, but also to give opportunities to those students who have a special interest in and ability with music.

Although music is now unquestionably part of the school curriculum it is also woven into the fabric of events in the wider community, frequently and necessarily taking place outside of conventional timetabled lessons in schools. I refer specifically to instrumental teaching schemes which operate through local authorities and are articulated by music advisers. Many of our young people find their richest musical experiences not in classrooms but rehearsing and performing in instrumental and vocal groups, often out of school time and sometimes out of school altogether. This activity has been largely staffed by peripatetic teachers working with small groups and individuals. Things are on the move here and we need to be vigilant in case these opportunities waste away by default.

An important element of music in schools is instrumental teaching. Music in schools for many parents, and certainly for the media, often seems to be instrumental lessons. In the secondary school, GCSE has already influenced the provision of specialist teaching, since musical *performance* is obligatory. By Key Stage 2 in the National Curriculum 'the need for specialist instrumental tuition becomes apparent'.[9]

This desirable state of affairs now comes into tension with contemporary school management. Each school is now responsible through its head teacher (manager) and the governing body for most of the decisions on spending and the budget. Local authorities are becoming educationally marginal and the instrumental services which they created may not be sustained by other agencies. Head teachers will have to consider whether this form of instruction is economically viable, when balanced against other things. Clearly, no school can provide a range of instrumental teachers to cover all the main options and effective schemes can only be operated in places by some new kind of federation, other local schools sharing the supply and funding of instrumental teachers. This is not likely to be a priority with school managers. And what about regional LEA based orchestras, bands and choirs? Will these still exist? We only have a Ministry of Education, unlike most European countries where there is also a Ministry of Culture to oversee community musical activities and monitor quality.

Policy on this seems hazy and there has been considerable agitation to try to make sure politicians understand what they are doing. One thing is certain, if these facilities disappear or are truncated then the rich British traditions of both professional and amateur music making will gradually be eroded and participation in instrumental and choral music will become even more exclusively the property of a better-off minority who need no persuading about the value of these things and can afford to pay.

In summary the *status quo* is as follows: music in schools is now essentially a practical activity; composing is widely practised and is generally thought to be both desirable and feasible; western staff notation is relegated to a supporting position in music learning, in the awareness that much music is notated in other ways and some not at all; singing, while thought desirable, does not seem to be as universally engaged in as it might be; it is deemed important to engage pupils in music from different cultural backgrounds; teachers distrust 'methods' and tend to devise their own materials; the two strands of music education – general and instrumental teaching – require greater organisational coherence.

Musical knowledge and the muddle of attainment targets

Fundamentally, the music teaching profession in both state and private schools has largely accepted that there are but three psychological avenues down which any of us can approach music; these are in the role of composer, performer, or audience listener. These are not an invention of educational theorists but wait to be discovered whenever we carefully reflect on the nature of musical experience. Recognising these three dimensions has been essential to recent music curriculum development and to the success of the GCSE, and this is acknowledged in the structure of the final music Report. The theoretical framework was explicated in the mid-seventies, principally in *A Basis for Music Education* by the present writer, along with the development of the important and related concepts of expressive and structural elements as essential musical features.[10]

The pervasiveness of this work can clearly be seen in the formulation of the attainment targets offered by the Working Group. After some initial confusion in the *Interim Report*, by August, 1991 we were offered the now familiar triad of elements which in effect define the fundamental activities of music as a school subject. These are proposed to be Composing, Performing and Appraising. The term appraising is carefully defined and refers specifically to the *audience-listener* role, which I previously carefully called 'audition' to distinguish this particular way of listening from what might be called composing-listening or performing-listening. In the Report it is tied in with what is called 'relevant knowledge' of historical and cultural backgrounds. Now, of course, appraisal also takes place when people are composing and performing and might often be best developed through these activities. However, at least a version of the concept of appraisal has been exposed and may prove helpful in justifying the knowledge basis of music to others and in clarifying the minds of music educators. The danger is that contextual, factual knowledge may be seen as central to musical knowing. It is seductively uncomplicated to manage in the classroom and relatively easy to assess. There are other ways of knowing entangled in musical experience and more must be said on this later.

Of course there are logical difficulties about this National Curriculum category set. Clusters of activities really cannot be attainment targets and composing, performing and appraising are essentially *activities*. What has been attained is surely what has been *learned*, the residue left with us, some change of insight, that which is taken away when an activity has, for the time being, ceased. In spite of this, the August 1991 document seems robust and rich enough in possibilities without being too prescriptive or limiting. We need to ask, though, whether educational reform will produce any significant change in the status and resource implications for music education.

Time and status under the National Curriculum

To get a feeling for the way in which music is regarded by those who are influential in curriculum policy we need to go back just one stage. The earliest statements on the subject basis of the National Curriculum occur in the DES consultative document of 1987[11] and the first Report from the

Task Group on Assessment and Testing (TGAT).[12] The consultative document lists three core and eight foundation subjects. Music appears at the end of the list of foundation subjects along with art and physical education. Between them all it is recommended they should take up around 10 per cent of curriculum time. These subjects are the last to be brought into the curriculum framework. Both the balance and sequencing reflect the *status quo* of earlier decades and do nothing to make it likely that there will be any radical change from earlier practice in terms of curriculum time and, by implication, allocation of resources.[13]

Assessment is surely the axis of the National Curriculum and here the status of music is once again analogous to that of art and physical education; there are merely to be 'guidelines' rather than specific attainment targets. It is obvious from this that these subjects are not considered to have a knowledge content sufficiently important or developed to merit any serious attempt at assessment. All this was highlighted by Angela Rumbold, then a Minister of State for Education, in a paper given to the National Association for Education in the Arts.[14] Her view of music education is informed and well expressed.

> 'Our aim will be to bring all pupils throughout their primary and secondary school years, into contact with the musician's fundamental activities in a wide range of different kinds of music - performing, singing or playing an instrument, or listening. I would hope that they would gain some experience of musical composition itself.'

This last sentence is interesting, especially the word 'itself'. This suggests that there is something refined, difficult or perhaps mysterious about the activity. This ambivalent attitude to composing permeates the whole consultative process. This may be implied in the letter from the Secretary of State, Kenneth Clarke, to the National Curriculum Council on 19 August, 1991, where he asks that 'to avoid an excessive degree of complexity and prescriptiveness ... I should like you also to consider whether there is a case for two attainment targets instead of three'.

Such a theoretical fixation on simplicity is sadly misplaced. Simplicity is not the same as effectiveness. If it were it might seem perfectly reasonable to reduce the essential three colours of red blue and green that make up a television image to two. Why not get rid of, say, red? Surely it would make television manufacture simpler? Unfortunately it would also compromise the level of visual reproduction in an unacceptable way.

In the Secretary of State's earlier response to the interim report he expressed concern for the many pupils 'with a real appreciation of music but a limited aptitude for its practice'.[15] It is clear from this that any shift towards two attainment targets would probably conflate composing and performing, thus shifting the balance away from practical experience. If either activity were thus to be diminished it would probably be composing, which is less understood by outsiders and less prestigious in the eyes of school communities than performing. It is easy to regard composing either as messing about in an aimless 'progressive' way or, conversely, as a process exclusively confined to the exceptionally talented, the Mozarts of this world. Considered either way, composing becomes problematic. To take a parallel case; it seems curious that experimentation in science or invention in technology is considered to be a curriculum essential for everyone, without any suggestion that pupils are just messing about or, on the other hand, that a PhD is required before anyone can undertake practical, scientific or technological investigation.

Even though it may be that the ultimate *aim* of general music education on schools is to promote an ability to respond to music in audience in a positive way, the process by which this end is achieved has for most pupils to be through practical involvement, when pupils engage in what Angela Rumbold called 'the musician's fundamental activities'. To argue that the an appreciation of music can be brought about just by listening in audience (even accompanied by relevant information) is analogous to saying that appreciating Shakespeare can be best achieved without any prior active involvement with the English language. This would be nonsense. Nor should we limit the scope of practical work to performing. As we have seen, composing music is something that most children have engaged in over the last decade and is certainly not a new element in British music classrooms. It is no rarefied activity but a way of engaging with the elements of musical discourse in a constructive and critical manner, making judgements and decisions; in the richest sense of the term, *appraising* music.

We also might also notice in the paper by Angela Rumbold, that music education is portrayed as a series of activities without reference to learning outcomes. Pupils are 'to gain experience of'; but to learn what? It is the view of music as knowledge or perhaps as *no* knowledge that pervades these attitudes to music in the curriculum and it is this central issue of music as knowledge that requires our attention.

The terms of reference for subject working groups spell out the concept of attainment targets as:

> '... the knowledge, skills, understanding and aptitudes which pupils of different abilities and maturity should be expected to have acquired at or near certain ages.'[16]

The emphasis here is quite rightly upon learning outcomes rather than activities as central elements of assessment. Further weight is given to these in the TGAT Report where the concept of 'profile components' is exposed.

> 'We recommend that an individual subject should report a small number (of) profile components reflecting the variety of knowledge, skills and understanding to which the subject gives rise.'[17]

Attainment targets are, then, to be seen as the specific elements making up profile components, which in turn are the fundamental strands of knowledge in a subject field. Unfortunately the early 'core' subject Working Groups proceeded to muddy the epistemological water. The English group came up with three profile components: Speaking and Listening; Reading; Writing. These are obviously categories of activities, not of learning outcomes. Mathematics formulated the following: Using and Applying Mathematics; Number, Algebra; Shape and Space; Handling Data. These are bunched up into two profile components: Number, Algebra and Measures; Shape, Space and Data Handling. We have here more or less the usual sections of existing maths curricula redefined for the new context. Science was initially credited with 17 attainment targets - such a lot of 'knowledge' here. They include activities such as 'Exploration of Science'. These mainly describe scientific topics for the classroom: Forces; Earth and Atmosphere, and so on. Such topics can hardly be the 'knowledge, skills, understanding and aptitudes which pupils of different abilities and maturity should be expected to have acquired' though they may well be projects through which this knowledge is gained.[18]

This general failure to identify the essential deep structures in 'core' subjects may not be surprising. Indeed, it might be inferred that teachers working in these subjects have been so protected by their traditional status and level of resource that there has been little pressure to think through the fundamentals of the epistemological structure, no urgency seriously to ask what are the essential knowledge dimensions, the real profile components of the subjects. The situation is very different in the arts areas. To fend off curriculum marginalisation and to find a compelling professional rationale, arts educators are endlessly turning over and disputing the nature and value of their particular activity, trying to articulate a 'philosophy', attempting to define the knowledge base.

Much of the difficulty in formulating a sensible curriculum for music stems from the complexity of different layers of knowledge involved in musical experience and the non-verbal nature of the activity. There is a long philosophical history lurking here which would be too complex and tedious to rehearse in this paper. Suffice to say that at times it is necessary for us to know *how* to do things, to operate a lathe, to spell a word, to translate a passage, to articulate our thoughts into a structured form, to manipulate a musical instrument, to use musical notation. Knowing how to do things is essentially the use and development of particular skills. The second commonly understood kind of knowledge is propositional, informational, knowing *that*. For example we may know that two plus seven makes nine, or that Manchester is 200 miles from London, or that '*avoir*' is the French verb 'to have', or that Beethoven wrote nine symphonies, or where rap originated. A further, though philosophically contested, way of knowing is that of knowledge by acquaintance. We may know Renoir's painting *The Rowers' Lunch*, or know a friend, a pupil or a city. Although such knowledge might to some extent be demonstrated by propositional statements, most acquaintance knowing is likely to be tacit, unarticulated. There is also an awareness of what we value, *attitudinal* knowledge which has been analysed by Bloom and others under the caption of the 'affective domain'.[19] The development of musical value positions relates to such variables as age, gender, social context, personality type and previous life experience, along with the accumulation of musical experience.

However we construe the epistemological map, *knowing* music is much more than processing factual information. In this the subject Working Group has been far from clear.

Appraising, musical analysis and musical knowing

It is in the context of musical knowing that the National Curriculum term 'appraising' becomes important. Although the term is specifically intended to pick up the skills and information context needed to respond to music as 'audience listeners', the implications are much wider. Appraising affirms that there is such a thing as musical *knowledge*. There are more or less objective musical criteria for critical judgements: musical appraisal is not a free for all. If this were not so it would be very difficult to justify music as a compulsory element of the curriculum and impossible to believe in any fair or meaningful system of assessment. If 'anything goes' then there will be no shared core of knowledge and therefore nothing to assess.

I have argued elsewhere that the development of musical criticism is the special contribution that schools and colleges can make to music education.[20] That is what distinguishes institutionalized music education from music encountered more casually on the street or in the media. Formal music education takes a special interest in critical statements that have *analytical* force, that say something about how a particular piece of music functions. All analysis is musical criticism but not all criticism is analysis. Analysis cannot be simply an expression of preference or a statement about the social or historical context of a piece of music but is essentially discourse about the internal functioning of a specific musical object. It is about the integrity of a particular work. Appraisal as a concept is interchangeable with analysis. It relies on first-hand acquaintance knowledge of particular musical objects. Anything less is either prejudice or inert information.

Musical appraisal is not necessarily promoted in verbal or scholarly ways. It can be elicited and developed at various levels; for example, in practical workshops where children are composing or improvising music. Here a teacher might ask questions to stimulate appraisal: 'What would the effect be if we played a cymbal here instead of a triangle?' 'What makes that passage sound so brilliant? 'Should this phrase be played quite so boldly or be more tentative in character?' 'Does this passage hold our attention when played so slowly (or so quickly)?' These kinds of question may be answered in practical ways, by musical experiment or demonstration, though verbal discourse is obviously important in any educational transaction and assists in the formation of critical judgement in music.

If we attend to music carefully and reflectively we shall find that there are four possible dimensions of critical appraisal or analysis. We might even call them profile components: 'the variety of knowledge, skills and understanding to which the subject gives rise'.

1. There can be appraisal of the sound *materials*, of the management of sonorities; of the 'soundscape' of a work, our impressions of timbre, texture, register, or loudness level.

2. There can be appraisal of *expressive character*; the general atmosphere of a piece, its dramatic levels, or the specific gesture of a single phrase.

3. There can be appraisal of *structural relationships*; the way expressive gestures relate to other gestures, how musical works undergo continual metamorphosis and in so doing keep us alert and attentive.

All three dimensions are areas where there can be objective critical judgements and where it is possible to be more or less right or wrong.

4. There can also be appraisal in terms of the *value of a work*; not simply a personal prejudice for or against opera or progressive rock as a genre, but an awareness for an individual listener of the significance of a particular musical encounter, a realisation built on the appraisal of materials, expressive character and structure. It is here that musical experience is at its most subjective and idiosyncratic.

These distinctions need to be clearly understood if meaningful assessment is to become a reality. Things can easily get confused. For example, the music Working Group lists 'structure' along with pitch, duration, chord or interval.[21] This is simply a category mistake, rather like placing the speech materials of vowels and consonants (speech is not necessarily meaningful) in the same conceptual level as the language elements of nouns or verbs (language is by definition always meaningful). Sound materials are to do with what we might loosely call musical *speech*. Expressive character and structure lie at the heart of musical *language*. They are qualitatively different from the perception and manipulation of sound materials.

It seems impossible to find any analytical or appraisal statement that does not fall into one of these four categories. This assertion can be tested quite easily by analysing any published review of musical performance into discrete statements. If we are really attending to music we are bound to assess the effect and control of sonorities, the management of the sound surface, the quality of the tonal experience itself; we are also conscious of the character of music, whether it is heavy, or light, flowing or angular; we may also look for coherence, ways in which musical gestures evolve, relate, contrast, or suggest or deny a sense of direction. We might also come to judge the place of a musical encounter in our own matrix of values, understanding its significance for us as human beings.

In our research in the Institute of Education, we have observed these modes of critical appraisal in the musical development of children.[22] A focus on sound materials characterises the early years. Up to about the age of three, young children appear to be primarily responsive to the direct impressiveness of sound phenomena, particularly timbre and dynamic levels. There is much experimentation with and exploration of musical instruments and vocal sound, though the children soon acquire techniques involved in handling sound, organising regular pulse and using technical devices suggested by the physical structure of instruments.

Expressive characterisation becomes most evident in compositions around the ages of four to six years. This becomes particularly apparent through the exploitation of changes of speed and loudness levels. Musical ideas at this time are often programmatic and the process of invention appeared to be quite spontaneous and unstructured. By seven or eight, most of the children we observed had gravitated towards established expressive musical conventions: marches, lullabies and so on. Phrases then tended to fall into standard two, four or eight bar units with regular metrical and standard tonal organisation.

Structural interest first emerges as musical speculation, usually between the ages of 9 and 11. Repetition of commonplace patterns is broken by imaginative deviations. Surprises occur as children deliberately explore structural possibilities, looking to contrast, overturn or vary musical ideas. Around 13-14, structural organisation becomes more firmly integrated into longer pieces in clearly identifiable idioms, especially though by no means exclusively from the realms of popular music.

At around 15 or so, particular pieces of music, often certain shapes of phrase or a harmonic progression become symbolically significant for an individual. There is a growing consciousness of music's emotional power and a tendency to reflect on this experience and to communicate something of the strength of these responses to peers. From the documentary evidence of musicians we can see how this significance may later become transformed into a value commitment revealed in novel composing techniques and original historical, musicological, psychological or philosophical work. Musical compositions may be based on sets of newly generated musical materials; note rows, and electronic series, and so on.

Development and assessment

This thumbnail sketch of musical development can offer insights into the knowledge contours of music. If we were to reconstitute the Key Stage statements of the National Curriculum in epigrammatic form within just one (simple!) dimension with reference to the pattern of children's musical development, we would have something like the following.

Key stage 1

Students should be able to recognise and identify different musical materials and use these skilfully to express an atmosphere or dramatic sequence.

Key Stage 2

Students should be able to distinguish and discriminate melodic and rhythmic devices found in songs and instrumental pieces and use these expressively.

Key Stage 3

Students should be able to draw attention to and exploit repetitions and contrasting musical ideas involving awareness of the expressive potential of harmony.

Key Stage 4

Students should be able to discriminate between various idiomatic practices and demonstrate this knowledge in their own musical work and through verbal articulation.

Most of the Key Stage statements in the National Curriculum document are essentially *quantitative* in character rather than *qualitative*. For example, at Key Stage 2, under the activity of performing, children should interpret 'more complex signs' while at Key Stage 3 they should interpret 'a variety of signs'. Generally, the progressive tendency throughout is towards 'more' independence, a 'greater understanding' of music and more 'sophisticated' ideas.

It is essential to recognise that any reliable form of assessment is dependent on the recognition of *qualitative* changes. We need to have criterion statements that pick up qualitative shifts; something more like recognising changes of gear in a car than trying to assess relative road speeds without adequate instrumentation. Inappropriate ways of assessing musical achievement certainly exist, for example GCSE procedures that involve giving marks for different categories - melody, harmony, texture and so on and then adding them up. This seems a curious way to engage in musical appraisal.

To give just one positive example, here are some draft criteria for assessing musical performance. Each one represents a change of quality. They have already been found useful and reliable.

Criteria for assessing musical performance
Level 1 - Sensory:

The performance appears to be fairly spontaneous, even erratic. Forward movement is unsteady and variations of tone colour or loudness appear to have no structural or expressive significance.

Level 2 - Manipulative

Control is shown by steady speed and consistency in repeating patterns. Managing the instrument appears to be the main priority and there is no evidence of expressive shaping or structural organisation.

Level 3 - Personal expressiveness

The general impression is of an impulsive and unplanned performance. Expressiveness is exhibited in changes of speed, accentuation and loudness levels. There is a lack of structural coherence.

Level 4 - The vernacular

The performance is tidy and expressive within accepted conventions and in a fairly predictable way. Melodic and rhythmic patterns are repeated with matching articulation and phrases are balanced.

Level 5 - The speculative

A secure and expressive performance includes some imaginative touches. Dynamics and phrase articulation are deliberately contrasted or varied to generate structural interest.

Level 6 - The idiomatic

There is a developed sense of style and an expressive vocabulary convincingly drawn from identifiable idiomatic practice. Technical, expressive and structural control are consistently and reliably demonstrated.

Level 7 - The symbolic

The performance demonstrates confident technical mastery, is stylistic and compelling. There is penetration into expressive and structural detail and a sense of personal commitment.

Level 8 - The systematic

Technical mastery totally serves musical communication. Form and expression are fused into a coherent and personal musical statement. New musical insights are imaginatively and systematically explored.

Further research based on the music-making of Greek children in Cyprus schools confirms that musical development takes place in the predicted sequence and that teachers are able to make confident judgements in assessing musical compositions at a high level of consensus, provided that they are helped by clear criterion statements.[23]

The weight of reporting on pupil progress in the National Curriculum would be considerably reduced if an analysis of the essential elements were the starting point in every subject. Further work is now in progress evaluating the reliability and validity of this approach, but it begins to appear that it may have something positive to offer music education as we try to gauge the effectiveness of school music under the National Curriculum. Indeed it is essential to develop sensitive, effective and economical means of assessment. There are indeed things to *know* in experiencing music and most of these are just not amenable to assessment by paper and pencil tests, any more than is knowing how to drive a motor car or splint a broken leg.

Sensitive music educators may be worried by all this, aware that there seems to be an exclusive focus on product rather than processes. Process and product are indeed terms that appear in the 1991 music curriculum document under the heading of assessment.[24] Let us not be misled by these terms and waste further time debating their relative importance. Products are simply what we make or say. Processes are invisible without products. There is no such thing as an 'end product' in education. To observe the process of an individual requires us to study a wide range of his or her products on more than one occasion. It seems unlikely that we shall or even ought to penetrate very far into trying to assess the processes of people. This would be presumptuous. Even Freud found certainty difficult under the relatively tranquil conditions of one-to-one discussion in his Vienna consulting room. In most classrooms such discernment seems implausible. But we *can* assess products.

It is the products of children, their *work* that we are able to assess in schools, *not* individual children as people. Once accept this important limitation of educational institutions and criterion statements can be seen to be both potentially fair and easy to use, provided that they are carefully devised, really sequential and their meaning clearly understood. We are also brought up with a jolt by this acknowledgement of the limitations of schools. They are just one agent in the education and development of children and can achieve certain things but not others. The most important knowledge may indeed be tacit, unvoiced. We do not, however, need to be sure about this in order to function effectively.

A rationale for music education

Beneath the surface details of the classroom and the curriculum lie important issues. That is why even music education is politically sensitive and why professors of philosophy elbow their way into the debate about the music curriculum. A teacher colleague once said that at a parents' evening he was accosted by the father of a pupil at school and asked two questions. Is there any value in music? Why is music in the school curriculum? In the few minutes available he had to formulate convincing answers. It is not uncommon for pupils too to want to know why music is in the curriculum. The first answer is the quick and immediate one. It runs something like this. Consider any cohesive community, what we call a culture. We shall find music. Sometimes it will be fused with ceremony, ritual, dance, story telling, even magic. At other times will be separated out into such entities as symphonies, pop songs or ragas. There is no need to defend the role of music. It is a valued activity in any culture. We may find it difficult to say *why* it is valued but we can certainly demonstrate *that* it is.

The more difficult question is the second. Why is music in the school curriculum? After all, it might be argued that there is plenty of music taking place in the wider community and that school is an inappropriate place for musical activities. Here the justification hinges on the quality of what is actually done in the school. There can be no case for music done badly. On the other hand, there is every justification for supporting music education when it is well done. Schools extend the scope of knowledge that is casually acquired elsewhere and there is a fund of human knowledge (perhaps better and more accurately designated as *knowing*) embodied in musical discourse that cannot be left to chance. If schools are to be regarded as basing their curricula on important and significant activities in any culture, then music is an obvious candidate, unless we happen to believe that the role of schools should be limited to certain basic activities such as reading, writing and arithmetic. If this is the case, then the school day could be radically shortened and the school leaving age lowered.

It is one thing to give answers at this level, it is another to understand the significance for professional practice. In order to be clear we need to strip away some dead wood of tangled 'philosophies' that have cluttered music education over the last decade or so. It will be necessary to be fairly cryptic in outlining these positions.

There are two apparently conflicting views that have confounded music education, dividing professional aspirations.

The first of these is the perspective that sees education primarily as the transmission of cultural heritage. Accordingly, people undergoing education, and especially children in school, are to be given information and skills that will enable them to participate in the accepted cultural conventions. This in turn helps to perpetuate and confirm the structure and content of the culture. The implications for music education are obvious. We would look for a growing familiarity with the master works, for an historical perspective on music, for factual knowledge about music and possibly skill with musical instruments, for a degree of musical literacy, for concert-going and record-buying habits. In the case of the student learning to play an instrument under specialist guidance, we hope we would be initiating him or her more rigorously into a long tradition of craftsmanship through a developed systems of instruction assessed by carefully graded examinations.

All of these activities can have immense value, but only if they are undertaken for better reasons than passing on the cultural heritage as though it were a kind of property or territory, and if they are seen in a stronger educational perspective. As it stands things often go wrong. Many students become alienated from the master-works and appear to collide with the cultural values that the teacher represents. If they acquiesce they may become knowledgeable about composers and their works without commitment to real experience of them. For the instrumental player, sensitivity is frequently obliged to go underground in deference to the acquisition of skills at a rate that exceeds the growth of musical understanding. Far too many students give up instrumental lessons than would be the case if there were something intrinsically satisfying in the activity. Furthermore, the quest for any common cultural heritage in multicultural settings seems doomed to failure and the most powerful musical experiences seem most frequently to occur outside of the constraints of formal education.

The second view, sometimes called 'progressive', is in sharp contradiction to the traditional picture, so rudely caricatured above. The central article of faith here is that we begin with the child as an unfolding personality and not a mere recipient of a culture. Accordingly, the emphasis is on learning rather than teaching, on the development of the imagination, on discovery and above all, on creativity. Thus, instead of accepting and perpetuating the *status quo*, we look for development of the ability to influence and change the culture. In music education we would place an emphasis on composition or improvisation, on experimentation with new sound materials, on small-group or individual activities rather than large choirs or bands. We would look for involvement with contemporary music, defined alternatively as either the music of contemporary composers or pop music. General music in schools is seen as very different from specialist instrumental tuition and the whole apparatus of examinations and tests becomes suspect because it imposes an unwelcome uniformity and in any case, attempts to measure the unmeasurable, the personal development of differing individuals. Is this why music is valued then: because it helps pupils develop as people in their own way?

Once again, the underlying assumptions of this theory may give rise to distortion of otherwise valuable activities and objectives. Teachers may even abdicate from teaching altogether in the interests of children 'discovering' for themselves, or from a misguided sensitivity to the creative processes of students. The music of the *avant garde* is not espoused by many and a good proportion of the students may feel that the school has no right to institutionalise popular music. The instrumental player goes his or her own way and shrugs off the low-level activity of the classroom, preferring to stay with the classical tradition, the rewards of examination passes and public acclaim. Worse still, most students may not seem at all interested in the development of their own personalities through music.

Following the philosopher Karl Popper, I would offer a less distorting perspective that signals the interactive nature of tradition and renewal and at the same time gives us a sense of direction.[25] This is derived from noticing a relationship between the two extreme views already examined. It is essentially human to be at once an inheritor, part of a culture, and an innovator, creatively striving within or against tradition. We assimilate the world to our own perspective but also accommodate to new realities. Each of us is moulded by the society in which we find ourselves but we also shape that culture through our individual actions. We are able to interact with the world precisely because we utilise such symbolic forms as language, maths, art and music. This symbol-making facility enables us to become aware of and articulate our personal history, the elements of our culture, the thought, the perceived feelings and actions of other people, the movement of planets, the natural world around us; all the forms and strands of human knowledge. It also allows us to speculate, to predict, to make attempts to shape the future. Symbol-making and symbol-taking are the supreme human gifts. The psychological space between one person and another, between an individual and the environment is mapped out through symbolic forms.

Music is one way in which people symbolically articulate their response to experience and share their observations and insights with others. It has something though not everything in common with the other arts, in that it is particularly well-adapted to illuminate those elements of human feeling which are fleeting and complex and the universal aspirations which most people share, whatever their culture.

Why we value music is ultimately not to do with belonging to a particular tradition or with self-development, but depends on a recognition that music is one of the great symbolic modes available to us. Initiation into this activity is what education is about. We might find ourselves drawn incidentally into a tradition or sub-culture, or may realise that we are developing as individuals: but these outcomes are by-products of doing music for its own sake, just as happiness is a by-product of something else, not a legitimate objective in itself.

No one has yet been able to explain in a totally satisfactory way how the arts function as symbolic forms, though many have tried. I shall not even attempt to open up that enigma here but simply note that musicians have taken extraordinary trouble to make sustained, complex and carefully articulated works and that people have responded to them as though they were significant, meaningful, symbolising something. Through them something is communicated, something is transmitted, something is known. When any work of art stirs us it is more than simply sensory stimulation or some kind of emotional indulgence. We are gaining knowledge and expanding our experience. The same is true when we form music as composers or perform it: the act of shaping music is a purposeful attempt to articulate something meaningful. It need not be complex or profound, earth-shattering or of cosmic proportions but it will be articulate, expressive and structured and just as 'objective' as the spoken or written word, an equation or a map.

The future

Children know how to learn. Schools can impede this impulse. We have to avoid the danger of predicating a curriculum upon a narrow view of musical knowledge and musical learning. In our studies of the musical development of children we have described a swing between assimilation and accommodation, between the personal world of the individual and the public domain of knowledge and experience 'out there'. The surface pleasure of sounds – the sensory – personal expressiveness and the experimentally speculative are all necessary energies and motivation flowing from the student. Acquiring aural and manipulative skills; entering the shared discourse of a musical vernacular and participating in idiomatic procedures are elements that schools and teachers can bring to the educational encounter. If we carefully observe what children actually do with music, we shall notice this constant crossing from one side of the other. The realities of human aspiration and development are not to be compromised or waylaid by apparently conflicting doctrines.

There is much to do now to equip primary school teachers to take on the role of music critic, to become sensitive appraisers, and to organise the music curriculum of primary schools in a planned, developmental sequence. This is where there are major resource implications and a need for imaginative teacher education. The main problem for secondary schools is that pupils arrive with radically different levels of ability and experience, often with diminishing enthusiasm for general music courses, and are grouped in classes of thirty. Options within music are essential to match the range of idiomatic engagement. The music curriculum may need to be thought of in a modular rather than a completely sequential way. The advantage of this is flexibility. Each project can be started at a level relevant to a group of pupils and using available expertise and resources. There can be culminating points, which may be a series of small-group performances, a whole class composition assembled from small-group contributions or a performance on record and tape of related items composed by children and 'professional' composers. A range of instrumental teachers and community musicians can and should be involved in this process. We must avoid any suggestion of perpetuating a separate musical sub-culture in schools, detached from music in the wider world.

However music in the curriculum is to be organised in the new framework, it will ultimately be defined, refined and managed by teachers supported by others in the field. Whitehall, Westminster and the National Curriculum Council have to acknowledge this. Through the Working Group a fairly serviceable structure has been articulated. Doubtless this could have been improved, for instance by moving towards outcomes statements as prime components when stating attainment targets, while specifying classroom activities as a second dimension. This is not to be. In January 1992 the National Curriculum Council, treating music in the same way as art, reduced the attainment targets to two, once again muddling up activities and outcomes – an elementary mistake that makes logical curriculum development difficult if not impossible. The Secretary of State's theoretical fixation with 'simplicity', revealed in his asking the NCC to consider whether there was a case for two attainment targets instead of three, has led to a conceptual mess. The NCC, by reducing music attainment targets to two, is committing an elementary error that makes coherent curriculum documentation difficult if not impossible. Performing and composing cannot be seen as targets standing separately in the same dimension as knowledge and understanding. Musical knowledge and understanding are learning outcomes that are fostered and *demonstrated* in these activities, and less clearly in audience-listening.

We were offered this framework:

Attainment target 1 – Performing and composing
The development of the ability to perform and compose music.

Attainment target 2 – Knowledge and understanding

The development of knowledge and understanding of musical history and theory, including the ability to listen to and appraise music.

The import of the NCC model, that knowledge and understanding have to be *about* music is simple nonsense. Knowledge and understanding can also be *of* music, directly experienced. Such rudimentary reasoning will push the school music curriculum back to chalk and talk that 15 years ago was making music so unattractive to pupils and will foster a belief in the value of acquiring inert information. If the NCC really wanted to go for simplicity, it could have settled for just *one* attainment target – *musical knowledge and musical understanding*, properly defined. The main curriculum activity strands can then be performing, composing and audience-listening.

This unprofessional piece of work, which seems to owe more to the dictates of politicians and civil servants than to an adequate understanding of the subject, has provoked a storm of protest, including responses from musicians such as the conductor Simon Rattle and the Chair of the Music Working Group. The integrity of the NCC is now seriously compromised.

Four leading professional associations, representing musicians and music education experts throughout the United Kingdom, have called on Kenneth Clarke, the Secretary for State, to reject the National Curriculum Council's advice that the music teaching in schools should have only two Attainment Targets, rather than the three recommended in 1991 by the National Curriculum Working Group for Music. The Incorporated Society of Musicians, the UK Council for Music Education and Training, and the Music Advisors' National Association, responded with concern to the NCC's Report, published on the 13 January 1992.

The following press release makes their position clear,

> The ISM, UKCMET, MANA, and SMA are dismayed by the NCC's advice to the Secretary of State for Education and Science that the National Curriculum for Music should have only two Attainment Targets – 'Performing and Composing' and 'Knowledge and Understanding' rather than the three – Performing, Composing and

Appraising – recommended last year by the authoritative National Curriculum Working Group for Music.

First, there has been a total disregard of the consultative process set up in relation to the Working Group reports, whose advice to the Secretary of State took into account the realities and successes of acknowledged advances in music education. The attempts by the NCC to interpret their own statistics which indicated that 80 per cent supported the Working Groups's recommendations – are demonstrably unconvincing.

Second, there is neither musical nor educational logic in favour of adopting only two attainment targets. The three targets recommended by the Working Group represent a means of achieving a broad and balanced musical education, as originally specified by the Secretary of State. The two targets preferred by the NCC lump together the important activities of performing music and composing; while seeking, for the sake of symmetry, to draw a spurious relationship between factual knowledge and the understanding of a subject. Parents will be more accurately and fully informed about pupils' musical knowledge and understanding if teachers assess these through the activities of performing, composing and appraising.

Third, while we take no exception to the end of Key Stage Statements, the Programmes of Study contain items which are totally inappropriate as a legal requirement. The worst of these misjudgements exist in Attainment Target 2, with its heavy emphasis on elements of musical history and theory. For example, at age 11 'recognise the distinctive characteristics of music from the following periods: medieval, renaissance, baroque, classical, romantic, recent and contemporary' and 'identify the characteristics of music from different styles and genres, including opera, ballet, folk and jazz and different cultures and traditions'.

Such prescriptiveness is contrary to the Secretary of State's terms of reference to the Music Working Group, which we endorsed, requiring the Group 'to advise on a statutory framework which is sufficiently broad and flexible to allow schools wide discretion in relation to matters to be studied'.

The citation of examples are also over-prescriptive and impractical to a point where we can have no confidence in the capacity of the National Curriculum Council as presently constituted, to formulate curriculum proposals and produce workable non-statutory guidance for classroom teachers of music.

Our associations are, of course, more than willing to co-operate in the development of the music curriculum and more into line with the Secretary of State's original intention of clarity and practicality.

In a letter from the author to the Secretary of State it was pointed out that the NCC was promulgating educational nonsense. The following formulation was suggested *(see Postscript):*

Attainment target 1 – Performing and composing
The development of the ability to perform and compose music with understanding

Attainment target 2 – Listening and appraising
The development of the ability to listen to and appraise music, including knowledge of musical history.

This was assimilated word for word into the Draft Order, though whether the professionals will now accept a two target model is questionable, especially since the Secretary of State has announced that these changes are more a matter of 'packaging' than of 'substance'.

What will happen now is, at the time of writing, very uncertain. It really is essential for politicians, civil servants, right-wing philosophers and other amateurs to withdraw. There are times when professional judgement has to be respected. Ultimately, curriculum development is teacher development and it is here that real curriculum change will be shaped and articulated, just as it always has been.

Keith Swanwick

POSTSCRIPT

The author sent a fax to the Secretary of State on 21 January 1992. The substance of this was carried by *The Times Educational Supplement* on the 24 January 1992. It was an attempt to place the music curriculum within a decent theory of musical knowledge and to push back the advancing tide of inert information implicit in the NCC's attainment target: 'Knowledge and Understanding – The development of knowledge and understanding of musical history and theory, including the ability to listen to and appraise music'.

The fax ran as follows,

Dear Secretary of State,

You will by now be aware of the widespread and profound disquiet over the NCC recommendations on the music curriculum. I write in the hope that action can be taken to avert professional alienation at the end of a process of committed consultation which appears to have been overturned by the NCC.

Without getting into unnecessary detail or subscribing to the appalling ideological warfare which has characterised some of the writing in the press, I shall identify the main difficulties and a possible way forward which would recover the confidence of musicians and music educators, on whom the future development of the music curriculum depends.

1. Attainment targets

The major impediment to professional acceptance of the report is the implication in the attainment targets that knowledge and understanding is essentially tied up with knowing *about* music and does not enter into performing and composing. This may not have been intended but it is inescapable in the way that the attainment targets are defined. Furthermore, the balance has been tipped heavily towards factual knowledge about music rather than knowledge of music by the actual wording of the second attainment target. This will have the effect of increasing the amount of factual information within a subject already restricted to a small corner of time in the school curriculum. Listening to music and appraising it is the key to understanding music history. It should not be slipped in at the end of the target statement after the word 'including'. The use of the word 'theory' is also misleading. I take it that this mainly means knowing about music notation, which is of course no substitute for being able to actually read and write music notation when composing and performing.

Clarification of the wording in the NCC's proposed attainment targets and the accompanying definitions would remove all of these objections and would, I believe, be supported across a wide spectrum of views.

AT1. Performing and composing
The development of the ability to perform and compose music with understanding.

AT2 Listening and appraising
The development of the ability to listen to and appraise music, including knowledge of musical history.

This formulation is logically, educationally, musically and practically acceptable and I would make every effort to persuade colleagues in the music and music education professions that it is so. If these ATs were to be given an approximate curriculum weighting of 60 (AT1) to 40 (AT2) the balance would be about right for most schools.

The programmes of study
There is specific concern about the second attainment target, especially at Key Stage 2. As it stands this is cluttered. There are four different items relating to different periods, styles and historical background. This is informational overkill for 8 to 11 year old children and would be impossible to sustain in the primary school music curriculum.

The examples
These are non-statutory and I hope they can be re-worked. Some are likely to be meaningless to many children and in any case, taken together they are culturally over-prescriptive.

Sincerely,

On Monday 27 January 1992, Kenneth Clarke, the Secretary of State, announced that he accepted this formulation of the attainment targets and agreed a weighting towards composing and performing of 2:1. Further work is expected during the consultation process on reducing the information load, especially during Key Stage 2. In the end, the advice of a 'professional' appears to have been of value in a confused situation of do-it-yourself curriculum writers intruding into an area without experience or expertise.

NOTES

1. Polanyi, M. (1967), *The tacit dimension*, London, Routledge.
2. See, Paynter, J. (1982), *Music in the secondary school*, Cambridge, Cambridge University Press.
3. An early considerated discussion of this issue is in Swanwick, K. (1968), *Popular music and the teacher*, Oxford, Pergamon.
4. Swanwick, K., (1977), Belief and action in music education, in Burnett, M. (ed.) *Music Education Review*, London, Chappell.
5. Swanwick, K., (1987) (ed.), *Music in schools: A study of context and curriculum practice*, London, Institute of Education.
6. The observation method was to record only those activities lasting for 5 minutes or more.
7. Department of Education and Science (DES), (1991), *Music for ages 5-16*, London, HMSO.
8. The term 'ethnic music' is used to indicate music from non-European musical traditions. The term is unfortunate and misleading, since all music is 'ethnic' in origin. However, at the time of the research it was in common use and was understood by teachers and others.
9. DES, (1991) *op. cit.*, p. 57.
10. Swanwick, K., (1979), *A basis for music education*, Windsor, NFER-Nelson.
11. DES, (1987a), *The National Curriculum 5-16*, London, HMSO.
12. DES, (1987b), *The National Curriculum Task Group on Assessment and Testing - A report*, London, HMSO.
13. As to the other arts, Drama is seen as part of English and Dance, a part of Physical Education.
14. Angela Rumbold October 1987, in The National Curriculum: Implications for the arts, *Take Up Series no.* 6 1988, National Association for Education in the Arts.
15. A letter from the Secretary of State for Education to Sir John Manduell, 14 February, 1991.
16. DES (1987a), *op. cit.*, Annex A.
17. DES (1987b), *op. cit.*, Section 35.

18. The Science attainment target 14, *Sound and Music*, seems very odd. It seems that music is to be defined in terms of pitched sounds. A tambourine and a side drum would presumably be ruled out as musical instruments and a police siren could be counted in.

19. Bloom, B. et al., (1964), *Taxonomy of educational objectives, Book 2, Affective domain*, New York, David McKay Co.
20. Swanwick, K., (1988), *Music, mind and education*, London, Routledge.
21. DES (1991), *op. cit.*, p. 7.
22. Swanwick, K. and Tillman, J., (1986), The sequence of musical development, *British Journal of Music Education*, Vol. 3, no. 3, Cambridge, Cambridge University Press.
23. Swanwick, K., (1991), Further research on the musical development sequence, *Journal of the Psychology of Music*, 19, p 22-23.
24. DES (1991), *op. cit.*, p. 45
25. Popper, K., (1972), *Objective knowlege*, Oxford, Clarendon Press.

MORE HAS MEANT WOMEN: THE FEMINISATION OF SCHOOLING

Jane Miller

'To an extent that is quite inadequately recognised, state education is provided by women; as is virtually all schooling, whether public or private, for young children.' Jane Miller argues that criticism of current educational practice often has gender as its hidden target. She draws on historical evidence and on her own teaching experience to develop a complex and provocative discussion.

WHAT WE KNOW ABOUT EFFECTIVE PRIMARY TEACHING

Caroline Gipps

Caroline Gipps looks at the findings of research and educational theorists on what are the most effective classroom practices and teaching methods in the primary school. Primary teachers faced with the introduction of the National Curriculum and related assessment, and calls from government ministers and others to move back to more formal methods in the classroom, will find here much to stimulate an examination of their practice, as well as encouragement to see the value and potential of their work.

THE ARTS 5-16: Changing the agenda

John White

John White critically examines the central issues that underlie the National Curriculum Council's document *The Arts 5-16: A curriculum framework*. Education in the arts has lacked a coherent sense of purpose and whilst the NCC has tried to provide an integrated policy it has paid insufficient attention to the underlying aims of education in the arts. In addressing this problem and presents a searching discussion of the purposes and underlying assumptions of education in the arts and their practical realisation. His concern is to ensure that the foundations for work in school in the arts are secure and defensible and above all will generate a love of art.

SCHOOL HISTORY TEACHING: Has the National Curriculum got it right?

Peter Lee, John Slater, Paddy Walsh and John White

The coming of the National Curriculum has left many questions unresolved about the aims of school history teaching and how these cohere with the aims of schools in general. Certain issues have attracted public attention, such as the weight to be given to British, as distinct from world, history, the relative weight to be given to learning the facts of history and to a broader understanding, and whether history should be optional after 14. But underlying these are deeper considerations. Why study history in school at all? Is it something to be engaged in for its own sake, or as part of education for citizenship? Is it just an expression of piety towards the past? Answers to such questions will determine attitudes towards and the content of history in the National Curriculum. The contributors to this London File paper - historians and philosophers - try to come to grips with these questions and comment on each other's views. The arguments and conclusions have important implications for the future of school history.

THE RIGHTS OF THE CHILD: Educational implications of the United Nations Convention

Susan Wolfson

The United Nations Convention on the Rights of the Child has profound and exciting implications for change in general educational ethos as well as for concrete educational reforms. Susan Wolfson discusses the ideological background to the Convention, the arguments on all sides of children's rights issues, and the correct balancing of those rights with states' responsibilities and parental entitlements. She examines the rights which children are denied by current educational practice, measuring them against the Convention's specifications article by article. She concludes that legal reforms as well as educational policy and practice changes must occur for states, parents and educationalists to fulfil their new responsibilities within the Convention, and for children fully to realize their new status within educational institutions and in their larger lives.

THE PROMISE AND PERILS OF EDUCATIONAL COMPARISON

Martin McLean

Education in other countries was rediscovered by government in Britain in the mid-1980s, after almost a century of neglect. Policy makers have made unprecedented appeals to foreign - apparently more successful - practice to support new policies. Does this reflect a new global order in which educational institutions must compete with international rivals just as fiercely as car manufacturers? Or is it a search for instant certainties in a world bereft of utopias, where everything is compared - students, teachers, schools, localities, countries and historical epochs - against slippery or specious norms? Martin McLean discusses the purposes, techniques and possibilities of cross-national educational comparison. He analyses international surveys of student attainment and of vocational education and the reports of the first twelve HMI expeditions to other systems. He argues that, properly done, comparison can enrich British education policy, but that, in too many cases, it has produced deceptive evidence which few have the means to check.

CHARTERS, CHOICES AND EDUCATIONAL RESPONSIBILITIES

Anthony Green

Anthony Green looks at the Citizen's Charter and the Parent's Charter, both issued by the Government in 1991. The 'charters' are political documents designed to appeal to voters, but they could well serve as the basis for legislation to come. They are also significant in their own terms as statements about rights and responsibilities in education. Central to them are the notions of informed choice, the restructuring of professional-client relations and 'value for money', as well as specification of parental rights and responsibilities. Anthony Green's aim is to present an analysis of the social, civil and political rights the charters seem to imply, and to develop discussion of the educational entitlements they endorse, deny and obscure.

SCHOOL HISTORY TEACHING: HAS THE NATIONAL CURRICULUM GOT IT RIGHT?

Peter Lee, John Slater, Paddy Walsh and John White

The coming of the National Curriculum has left unresolved questions about the aims of school history teaching and how these cohere with the aims of schools in general. Certain issues have attracted public attention; the weight to be given to British, as distinct from world, history, the relative weight to be given to learning the facts of history and to a broader understanding, and whether history should be optional after 14. But underlying these are deeper considerations. Why study history in school at all? Is it something to be engaged in for its own sake, or as part of education for citizenship? Is it just an expression of piety towards the past? Answers to such questions will determine attitudes towards and the content of history in the National Curriculum. The contributors to this London File paper - historians and philosophers - try to come to grips with these questions. Their arguments and conclusions have important implications for the future of school history.

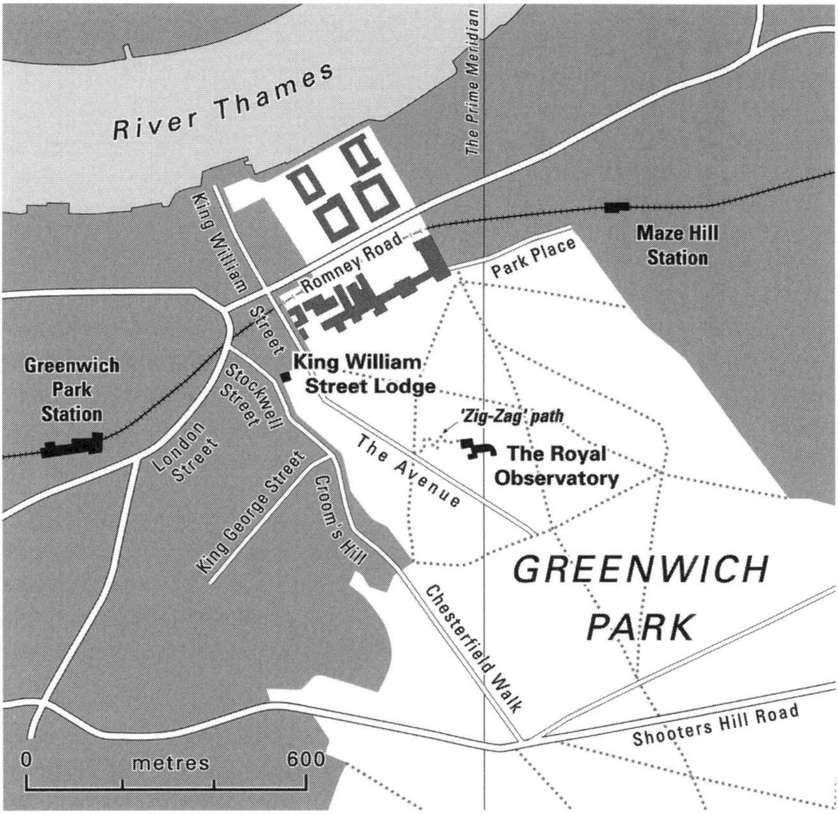
River Thames
The Prime Meridian
King William Street
Romney Road
Park Place
Maze Hill Station
Greenwich Park Station
King William Street Lodge
Stockwell Street
London Street
'Zig-Zag' path
The Royal Observatory
The Avenue
King George Street
Croom's Hill
GREENWICH PARK
Chesterfield Walk
Shooters Hill Road
0
metres
600

Martial Bourdin and lady (unidentified) by courtesy and kind permission of Mark Samuels, great-grandson of H. B. Samuels